GOD'S BENEFIT:
HEALING

God does want you well!

HARRISON HOUSE
Tulsa, Oklahoma

Unless otherwise indicated,
all Scripture quotations are taken from
the *King James Version* of the Bible.

06 05 04 03 02   24 23 22 21 20 19

God's Benefit: Healing
ISBN 0-89274-228-3
Copyright © 1981 by Marilyn Hickey
P.O. Box 17340
Denver, Colorado 80217

Published by Harrison House, Inc.
P. O. Box 35035
Tulsa, Oklahoma 74153

GOD'S BENEFIT:
HEALING

One of the most important things to be considered when choosing a job is the benefits offered. Employers talk about "fringe benefits," "health benefits," "dental benefits," "maternity benefits," "travel benefits," and others. A good question to ask, whether you're applying for a job or maybe even considering an insurance policy, is, "What are the benefits?"

I like this definition for "benefit": "anything contributing to an improvement in condition." A benefit should improve our condition! That's why we like all those benefits—because they make things better for us.

Do you know that God has benefits for His children? He does! They're benefits that really improve our condition. Psalm 68:19 says, "*Bless-ed be the Lord, who daily loadeth us with benefits....*" Two of those benefits are listed in Psalm 103:2-3: "*Bless the Lord, O my soul, and forget not all his benefits: Who forgiveth all thine iniquities; who healeth all thy diseases.''* Aren't those two wonderful benefits? I don't know of any employer who offers benefits like those!

Would you ever work for someone and not accept their benefits? That wouldn't be very smart, would it! We'd never consider doing something like that in the natural; but I want you to know, there are many people who refuse God's benefits!

People say to me, "I don't believe it is God's will to heal everyone," or, "I don't believe this is the dispensation for healing." But if you're a child of God, one of the benefits of that relationship is healing for your physical body. ". . . forget not all his benefits . . . Who healeth all thy diseases."

Human nature is funny to me. In the day that Jesus walked upon the earth, the Pharisees didn't become upset over His healing of the sick; they became upset about His forgiveness of sins. In our day it's just the opposite! People don't become upset when you say that Jesus forgives sins, but mention that Jesus heals sickness and they really get "up-tight." Actually, it's the same old enemy, fighting against the full message, the entire Good News, of what Jesus wants to do for mankind. God wants to forgive us of our sins, thus allowing Him to give us a new life and

4

nature; and He also wants to heal our physical body. Don't forget *all* His benefits!

Psalm 103:3 is very revealing. It shows how forgiveness and healing go hand in hand: "*. . . Who forgiveth all thine iniquities; who healeth all thy diseases.*" They shouldn't be separated!

In the New Testament, the Greek word SOZO is translated "save" and "heal." In Mark 5:23 Jairus asked Jesus to lay hands on his sick daughter, "*That she may be healed.*" And in Acts 2:47 it is recorded that "*. . . the Lord added to the church daily such as should be saved.*" SOZO is the Greek word used in both verses. It is used interchangeably to mean "save" or "heal." Since we know it is God's will to forgive sins and save, we must also accept the fact that it is His will to physically heal and make whole.

Healing is not something new. God's healing begins in the Old Testament and flows throughout the New Testament. It continues to flow today! I always take the overall view of the Bible on any topic. Some people say that they just like to study the New Testament, and some people like to study the Old Testament. I like to study both because then I think I get the full message of what the Lord is trying to say to me.

THE HEALING LAMB

Healing begins to flow in the Old Testament in Exodus 12. Do you remember the account of the passover lamb? The whole family ate of the lamb, and the Bible tells us that when the destroyer came, he passed over the households where the blood of the lamb was seen on the door posts, where the people had partaken of the lamb.

The blood on the door posts saved the people from the destroyer. After eating the lamb, the Bible says they left Egypt in great physical strength and with good health (Psalm 105:37). God took away sickness from the midst of them (Exodus 23:25).

Why did they not have any sickness? The reason, I believe, was because they were full of lamb. When you are full of the Lamb, I believe you receive strength and health. They ate of that lamb, and there was no sickness in their midst. The Bible talks of elderly people who marched out of Egypt in great strength and divine health. Partaking of the lamb was not only for their forgiveness, it was not only to protect them from the destroyer, but it was also to give them strength and health.

Look to Jesus as your healer, but also look to Him as your strength—physical strength. Joel

3:10 says, "... *let the weak say, I am strong.*"
And David, in Psalm 29:1 says, *"The Lord will
give strength unto his people...."* We have
begun to see the unfolding of it. God saved His
people from the destroyer (the devil) and gave
them physical health and strength.

HEZEKIAH'S HEALING PRAYER

II Chronicles 30 relates how Hezekiah renewed
the passover. The Israelites had not been eating
the passover, and when it was renewed, the king
prayed for the sick *"And the Lord harkened to
Hezekiah, and healed the people"* (II Chronicles
30:20). It was in the eating of the passover and in
the king's praying that the nation was healed.
Once again the lamb was connected with healing.
The Lamb of God brings forgiveness *and* healing.

HEALING FOR THE LEPER

Cleansing was provided for the leper, and the
preparation for cleansing included the slaying of
a lamb. Leviticus 14:25 says, *"And he [the priest]
shall kill the lamb of the trespass offering, and
the priest shall take some of the blood of the
trespass offering, and put it upon the tip of the
right ear of him that is to be cleansed, and upon*

the thumb of his right hand, and upon the great toe of his right foot."

The lamb brought salvation to the Israelites from their Egyptian oppressors, and the lamb also brought cleansing to them when they needed healing. The lamb that brought deliverance was the same lamb that brought wholeness. When we partake of the Lamb of God, we enjoy salvation and healing. The same Lamb provides both benefits!

HEALING IN THE WILDERNESS

God wants His people well, but it is up to us to make the decision to walk in health. One thing that works *against* good health is murmuring. Numbers 16 records how the Israelites murmured against Moses and against Aaron. Verse 49 says that 14,700 people died in the plague that followed the murmuring. The Bible says that a lot more were going to die, but Aaron made intercession as a priest, and stopped the plague. Jesus is our great High Priest, and He has come down to the people to stop the plague of sin and sickness. He does not want us to be sick. He wants us to be healed. He wants to improve our condition.

There was another time that the Israelites mur-

8

mured. Numbers 21 tells of how "... *the people spake against God, and against Moses....*" Fiery serpents came against the people and began to bite them. The people became sick and were dying. The Lord gave Moses a remedy: *"Make a brass serpent, Moses. Put it high on a pole, and everyone who looks at it will be healed."*

Jesus referred to that incident when He said, *"And as Moses lifted up the serpent in the wilderness, even so must the Son of man be lifted up ..."* (John 3:14). Everyone who looks to Jesus will be saved eternally. When we lift up Jesus as Savior, He heals people of sin; and when we lift Him up as Healer, people are healed physically, just as the Israelites were healed physically.

If people are not being healed in your church, maybe it is because Jesus is not lifted up as Healer. If those people in the wilderness hadn't looked up to the serpent, they would not have been healed. If you don't look up to Jesus to be your Healer, you will remain sick and in pain. It is very, very important that He be lifted up as Healer, as well as Savior.

HEALING IN THE PSALMS AND PROVERBS

"Bless the Lord, O my soul, and forget not all

*his benefits: Who forgiveth all thine
iniquities; who healeth all thy diseases; Who
redeemeth thy life from destruction; who
crowneth thee with lovingkindness and
tender mercies; Who satisfieth thy mouth
with good things; so that thy youth is renewed like the eagles" (Psalm 103:2-5).*

You don't have renewed youth unless you have
good things in your mouth. If you murmur, you
are going to be sick and cut short your life span,
and you will be weak while you are alive. But if
you speak good things (who Christ is; what He's
done) the benefits are that He forgives your iniquities, He heals you of disease, He redeems
your life, He crowns you with lovingkindness and
tender mercies, He satisfies you with good
things, and He renews your youth. Those are the
benefits of Jesus! Don't neglect any of them.
Don't say, "Well, He forgave me of my sins—
that's enough." Take them all. They're all your
benefits. Step up for every one of them!

*"My son, attend to my words; incline thine
ear unto my sayings. Let them not depart
from thine eyes; keep them in the midst of
thine heart. For they are life unto those that
find them, and health to all their flesh" (Pro-
verbs 4:20-22).*

God has given us the Word to bring life and to

bring health. We have the heavenly prescription for good health: attend to the Word by listening to it (which implies obeying it), reading it, and meditating on it. God is always wanting to improve your condition by giving you health for all your flesh.

If you are not in the Word every day, if you are not confessing the Word, I don't believe that you have that health flowing through you all the time. Jesus said, *"My words are spirit and they are life."* If you are not using the Word, then I do not believe that you have that life flowing in you all the time. I think that is one reason why Christians decay and fall apart, because they haven't kept the life principle of the Word in them *all the time.*

Have you noticed that sometimes when you get up in the morning the devil really hits you? Maybe you had a bad dream, or things were not going very well, and the enemy talks to you and says, "This day is going to be a drag. It's going to be terrible. You've got all these things to do, and everything is falling apart around you."

When that happens, I pray and go through the Scriptures that I'm confessing that day. After I'm through confessing the Word, there is something of *life* that begins to go around inside of me. Then I think, "This isn't a bad day. This is the best day of my life!" The Word has brought *life* into the situation. That's a wonderful principle, and we need to exercise it every day.

HEALING IN THE NEW TESTAMENT

Very early in His ministry, Jesus stood up in the synagogue to read. He was handed the book of Isaiah and read: *"The Spirit of the Lord is upon me, because he hath anointed me to preach the gospel to the poor; he hath sent me to heal the brokenhearted, to preach deliverance to the captives, and recovering of sight to the blind, to set at liberty them that are bruised, To preach the acceptable year of the Lord"* (Luke 4:18-19).

He said that He was *". . . To preach the acceptable year of the Lord."* What is *"the acceptable year of the Lord"*? I believe it refers to the year of Jubilee, mentioned in Leviticus 25. Every fiftieth year the trumpet was sounded and liberty was proclaimed throughout all the land. Everyone who owed debts and everyone who was in trouble was set free to go back and claim their own land. It was a beautiful time when everyone celebrated.

When Jesus stood up and said, "This is the acceptable year of the Lord," He was saying, "This is Jubilee! You can claim back all your possessions that Adam lost to Satan." The broken-hearted could be healed, the captives could be set free, the blind could receive their sight, people who were bruised emotionally could be set free. Jesus was standing up, and, in a sense, blowing a trumpet and saying, "This is Jubilee! There's Good News! Get back all your possessions that you lost in Adam. I've got them all back for you." One of those possessions is divine health. Jesus got it back for you. Claim healing as your rightful possession.

HEALING'S PRICE

You have every legal right to claim your healing, and I want to consider this carefully. In Matthew 8:17 there is a reference all the way back into Isaiah 53. Jesus had just physically "... *healed all that were sick*..." in that area, and the Bible says He healed them *"That it might be fulfilled which was spoken by Isaiah the prophet, saying, Himself took our infirmities, and bare our sickness."*

Isaiah, speaking of the suffering Savior, said, *"But he was wounded for our transgressions, he was bruised for our iniquities: the chastisement of our peace was upon him; and with his stripes we are healed"* (Isaiah 53:5). On the cross, Jesus paid the price for our transgressions. It was on the same cross and by the same suffering that Jesus paid the price for our healing. We have every legal right to forgiveness of sins because Jesus bore our sins for us. We have the same legal right to healing because Jesus bore our sickness and carried our diseases.

Do you believe it? Are you sure it's true? Healing must be believed and received, just as forgiveness of sins must be believed and received. The reason I know that is true is found in the first verse of Isaiah 53: *"Who hath believed our report? and to whom is the arm of the Lord revealed?"* Are you going to receive this report, or are you going to turn it down? Receive it today!

A CAUSE OF SICKNESS

In the New Testament, many people were sick because they did not discern the Body of Christ (I Corinthians 11:30). Paul, under divine inspiration, said that they were sick and weak because they were not properly discerning the Body of the Lord Jesus, and, as a result, many of them died early.

It is in the Body of Jesus Christ that we find strength and healing. It is God's will that we, as

14

part of the Body of Christ, enjoy the life and health that is in that Body. You expect forgiveness in that Body, and if you'll discern that there is also healing in that Body, you can have it. Properly discern the Lord's Body when you take communion, and you'll enjoy life and health.

Paul gives the best description of the Last Supper of any of the writers in the Bible. The gospel writers give us some description, but Paul gives the best—even though he wasn't there! How did he know so much? The Bible says he received it by revelation. That's revelation knowledge. God wants us to receive by revelation the knowledge that His Body has forgiveness and healing.

HEALING IN A NAME

If we understand who Jesus is, then we will better understand His Body. Names are very important in the Bible. The compound names of Jehovah in the Old Testament correspond to Jesus in the New Testament and help us discern the Body of Christ. There are seven names:

JEHOVAH-SHAMMAH: It means "the Lord is there." Jesus said, *"Lo, I am with you always, and I will never leave you"*; therefore, Jesus is Jehovah-Shammah.

15

JEHOVAH-SHALOM: Jesus is our peace. Shalom means "peace." Jesus said, *"My peace I give unto you...."* Part of redemption is having the presence of the Lord.

JEHOVAH-RAAH: "The Lord my Shepherd." Jesus says, *"I am the Good Shepherd."*

JEHOVAH-JIREH: "Jireh" came about as a revelation on Mt. Moriah. God said that He would provide a lamb for Himself. On Mt. Calvary, Jesus offered Himself as the Lamb for the sins of the world. Jehovah-Jireh means, "The God who sees ahead and provides." Jesus is the provision for redemption.

JEHOVAH-NISSI: It means "victory." Paul said, *"Now thanks be unto God which giveth us the victory through our Lord Jesus Christ."* Jesus is our victory.

JEHOVAH-TSIDKENU: "God our righteousness" in the Old Testament is Jesus our righteousness in the New Testament. I Corinthians 1:30 says, *"Jesus is made unto us wisdom, righteousness, sanctification and redemption."*

JEHOVAH-RAPHA: It means "the Lord my Healer." Jesus took our sicknesses and our diseases. In His redemptive work, He is the Lord our Healer. The Old Testament constantly revealed God as the one who healed in many ways.

METHODS OF HEALING

The Bible records a number of different methods used to bring about healing. We use the same methods today. Sometimes we lay hands on the sick and there is an instant miracle. Other times we lay hands on the sick and they don't appear healed—it doesn't seem that they have received an immediate miracle. Sometimes we have people lay hands on us and we get better a little at a time.

Remember the little boy in the gospels who *"began to get well"* (John 4:52) when Jesus spoke the Word? The mending seemed to take a period of time. Don't be discouraged if you don't see or feel something instantly. The Bible says that believers *". . . shall lay hands on the sick, and they shall recover."* Sometimes it seems that you must stand on the Scriptures until you almost think it is taking an eternity to recover!

I remember when the Lord promised us a child.

17

I had gone to many doctors, fertility experts, and they all said that I could never have a baby. But my husband and I never agreed with those words. We believed that God wanted us to have a child.

When we first started in the ministry, we were in Dallas, Texas, where a man named William Branham was ministering. One night I stood on the platform before him, and he looked at me and said, "You're not from here. You are from a wooded area. You are from Denver, Colorado, and you have a female condition." All the time he was speaking I had the most unusual sensation. I saw something in my spirit (not with my physical eyes), and I felt something that went round and round. It was whirling. It was almost like I could hear the sound of it. As it became stronger and stronger, I thought, "If I step into that, I will die." It was a fearful thing to me.

The evangelist said, "Go home and receive your baby," and that whirling (I believe it was the presence of God) went into my feet and came up into my body. A very unusual experience!

"Well, did you get your baby that year, Marilyn?"

"No, we didn't get the baby until ten years later!"

My husband never quit believing. He always

18

said, "Marilyn, God is going to give us a child."
When I began my thirties, I thought, "Forget it,
God. Don't listen to my husband. Listen to me."
But Wally stood in faith, and when I was thirty-
six, I went to a doctor because I was having some
unusual things happening in my body.

"You're not pregnant," he told me. "You're
just going through 'the change.' Don't even tell
your husband that you think you're pregnant."

I waited a few more months (I would have been
about four-and-a-half months along by then), and
I was having some more changes. I thought,
"Somebody's wrong!" After a check with
another doctor, I was told, "Lady, what you are
feeling is life. You are pregnant." At last Sarah,
our miracle baby, was born.

What am I saying to you in all of this? When
you don't see it, do you quit believing? When you
don't feel it, do you leave it alone? No! But you
say, "Ten years!" Well, Abraham waited twenty
years, and look what he got—an Isaac. There are
times when it seems that you wait and wait and
wait. (I didn't wait, but my husband did!) Don't
cash in on your faith!

Another time I had a back ailment. Every time
I picked up something heavy I would be in terri-
ble agony. Finally I went to a doctor and he took
X-rays of my back and told me, "You have the

19

strangest spinal formation I have ever seen. As you get older, it will get worse. You can't pick up anything heavy because you won't be able to walk if you do."

Once again I didn't receive the report. After I went home and told my husband, he agreed with me in prayer that I was healed. I stood on Mark 11:24, and you know what? I got worse! I got worse almost every day. I had to get out of bed at night and sleep on the floor because of the pain.

Sarah was just a baby then, and I'd pick her up, and she'd be heavy which would make my back worse. Every day I'd say, "According to Mark 11:24 I believe I have received." I didn't say the symptoms weren't there, and I didn't say there was no pain. I just said, "I believe I have received." At the end of six months, without anything dramatic happening (no cloud or warm glow or anything) I just stood up one morning, and I was all right. I stood on that Scripture for a long time, and God brought it to pass; however, there have been other times when I've had prayer and instantly been healed.

When my husband and I started our church, I had a tiny growth on my finger, and it was the ugliest thing! I went to church one day and showed it to one of the ladies in the church.

"Oh dear," she said. "I had a friend who had

some of those come on her fingers, and it was cancer, and she died."

Thanks a lot! That was a great help to my faith! But in a service one night I said, "God, I'm not going to have that any more." It began to turn dark on my finger during the service, and when I got home, it fell off. Whether it is an instant miracle or a recovery, God still wants to heal!

HEALTH AND OLD AGE

Some people will look for any excuse to be sick! They will say, "Well, you know, your body just wears out when you get older, and you're bound to be sick." Really? Let's read what the Bible says:

"The days of our years are three score and ten" (Psalm 90:10a).

"O my God, take me not away in the midst of my days" (Psalm 102:24).

"Why shouldest thou die before thy time?" (Ecclesiastes 7:17b)

"Well, Marilyn, if people never get sick, how are they going to die? They can't live forever."

The Word says, *"Thou takest away their breath, they die, and return to their dust"* (Psalm 104:29b). God can take away your breath and you

21

just go, and that's it! The Old Testament doesn't talk about the patriarchs dying in agony with a big cancer on each side of their head. It says, *"They gathered up their feet and were gathered up to their people."* That was it. They seemed to know when they were going to die.

Paul, in the New Testament, said, "You know, I'd really like to die; I would far rather go on, but I've made a choice that you need me more. I'm going to stay around a while longer." Paul believed that he had authority over his life span. And I do too! I'm just that radical. I believe that there is a life span that we can have, and when it is time, we can say, "OK Lord, I believe that I've fulfilled what You told me to do. I'm willing to go on now." At that time I believe He can take our breath, and we'll be gone.

I don't believe that we are to die in defeat. It bothers me when I see Christians suffering, and I don't believe that you should wait until you are seventy years old to start claiming strength for your old age. I think that every day you should thank God for the *"law of the spirit of life in Christ Jesus"* that sets you free from the law of sin and death.

Start planning and planting right now for your older years to be strong and healthy. Don't wait. That doesn't mean that you can break all of the health rules either. People who do not brush their teeth are going to get cavities. You can't say, "I just gave up that old devil toothbrush." I think you should take care of your body, feed it properly, and give it rest. I also believe that we should thank God every day for the divine health that flows through us. We should still be at our best at the time the Lord calls us home. We can say, "OK Lord. I've completed Your plan for me. Take me home. I'm ready to go." Don't go sick— go in health!

HEALING AND THORNS

There's another favorite excuse people like to use to justify staying sick—Paul's thorn in the flesh. I want to discuss Paul's thorn, but most of all I want to tell you, "Don't look for excuses!" When you are believing for healing, and people come to you with negative reports, don't receive them into your spirit. I don't think you have to slap the person down and say, "Shut up! I don't want to hear you." But I think you can say in your own spirit, "I just don't receive this. This isn't mine. I'm not going to take this into my spirit. I'm standing on the Word, and I believe that I have received."

When you begin to walk in faith in the area of

healing, the devil will test you and test you. Sometimes people will bring certain Scriptures to you, and they'll say, "See, it isn't always God's will to heal!" One thing they will always bring up is Paul's thorn in the flesh. I'm going to expose the devil right now so that he can't use Paul's thorn to create doubt in your mind and cause you to not believe God for your healing.

The first thing we need to do is read the Bible instead of listening to what other people say about Paul's thorn. Carefully read II Corinthians 12:7-10:

"And lest I should be exalted above measure through the abundance of the revelations, there was given to me a thorn in the flesh, the messenger of Satan to buffet me, lest I should be exalted above measure. For this thing I besought the Lord thrice, that it might depart from me. And he said unto me, My grace is sufficient for thee: for my strength is made perfect in weakness. Most gladly therefore will I rather glory in my infirmities, that the power of Christ may rest upon me. Therefore I take pleasure in infirmities, in reproaches, in necessities, in persecutions, in distresses for Christ's sake: for when I am weak, then am I strong."

Now, people will say, "See Marilyn, he was

sick! And God didn't remove his sickness because His grace was sufficient. And sometimes more glory is given to God for people to be sick and endure it and be sweet before the Lord than if they got healed." Have you ever heard that story? Maybe you told it in the past! I know that I have visited with some in the past, and they have said, "Well, I'm a real blessing being sick like this because people come here and I can comfort and strengthen them." Sometimes people say, "I went to pray for sister Jones, and she was so sick. But, when I left, she had ministered to me. I just wonder if her sickness wasn't in the will of God so that she could show how she endured illness in Jesus."

Those are all suppositions. When you begin to rationalize, you find yourself in trouble with the Word of God. You can end up rationalizing away God's promises! I know because I have done it. It happens like this. You think, "Well, if Paul had a thorn in the flesh, and he's more spiritual than I am, then I suppose sickness is my thorn, too." Don't rationalize the Word. Don't "suppose" yourself into being sick! Before you go confessing something about sickness, you had better know what the Word really says!

The best way to understand the Bible is to let the Bible interpret the Bible. Doesn't that make sense? The Bible tells us very plainly what Paul's thorn was. Paul knew the Old Testament intimately. He had memorized great portions of it. Old Testament examples and quotes and expressions are abundant in his writings. In II Corinthians 12 Paul uses an Old Testament expression to describe what it was that was given to him. Read Numbers 33:55: *"But if ye will not drive out the inhabitants of the land from before you; then it shall come to pass, that those which ye let remain of them shall be pricks in your eyes, and **thorns in your sides**, and shall vex you in the land wherein ye dwell."*

And Joshua 23:13: *"Know for a certainty that the Lord your God will no more drive out any of these nations from before you; but they shall be snares and traps unto you, and scourges in your sides, and **thorns in your eyes**, until ye perish from off this good land which the Lord your God hath given you."*

And Judges 2:3: *"Wherefore I also said, I will not drive them out from before you; but they shall be as **thorns in your sides**, and their gods shall be a snare unto you."*

What, according to the Bible, are thorns? Sickness? No! Thorns are people. Now go back to

26

II Corinthians. What are thorns? They are simply people. Did you ever have some people who were thorns to you? Maybe a nasty relative! Scripturally speaking, thorns are people, not sickness.

Paul describes what the thorn was doing. "It was the messenger of Satan to buffet me." Buffet means "to hit." And messenger here means "an angel of Satan." A fallen angel was coming along and beating on him.

Ananias prophesied when he met Paul. He said, "Paul, you're going to suffer many things for the name of Jesus. You're going to be persecuted." And sure enough, every place that Paul went he was persecuted. They physically hit him, they stoned him, they beat him. Who was inciting all those things? Satan. Paul saw behind the people and knew that Satan was behind the persecutions.

The Bible does say that Paul was sick at the beginning of his ministry (Galatians 4:13), but the Bible also says that at the end of his life he said, "... *I labored more than all of them....*" That doesn't sound like a very sick man, does it? It sounds like he was healed and went on to labor for the Lord.

Some say that Paul had an eye disease and that he had running pus coming from his eyes. But the Bible doesn't say that! The Bible says in Acts that people took aprons from Paul's body and put them on the sick and they were healed. Paul had divine health flowing through him!

Paul said, *"Most gladly therefore will I rather glory in my infirmities...."* Was Paul speaking of sickness there? According to Vine's Expository Dictionary, infirmities means "want of strength, weakness, indicating inability to produce results." Paul was rejoicing in his own inability to do anything for the Lord. *"... for when I am weak, then am I strong" (II Corinthians 12:10).* Paul listed his infirmities in II Corinthians 11:23-30 and never once listed sickness! We need to know these things so that the devil has no ground to put sickness on us!

No matter how much you talk to some people, they'll still fight to keep their sickness. Even if you convince them from the Scriptures that Paul's thorn was not sickness, they'll still say, "Well Marilyn, I just don't think that it's God's will to heal everyone." I want to let you read what the Bible says about that. The Word is very clear regarding God's will to heal all. Jesus is God's will in action (John 5:19). What did Jesus do when confronted with sickness?

"And Jesus went about all the cities and villages, teaching in their synagogues, and

preaching the gospel of the kingdom, and **healing every sickness and every disease** *among the people" (Matthew 9:35).*

I want you to have so much Scripture, and so much faith in the Word, that you would be ashamed to be sick anymore. Does that Scripture say that He healed some sickness? No, He healed *every* sickness and *every* disease.

"And when he had called unto him his twelve disciples, he gave them power against unclean spirits, to cast them out, and to heal **all** *manner of sickness and* **all** *manner of disease" (Matthew 10:1).*

"But when Jesus knew it, he withdrew himself from there; and great multitudes followed him, and he healed them all" (Matthew 12:15).

Is it His will to heal part of the people? To heal how many? ALL!

"And Jesus went forth, and saw a great multitude, and was moved with compassion toward them, and he healed their sick" (Matthew 14:14).

It doesn't say He just healed part of them. It says, "... *he healed their sick.*"

"And when the men of that place had knowledge of him, they sent out into all that country round about, and brought unto him all that were diseased, And besought him that

29

they might only touch the hem of his garment; and as many as touched were made perfectly whole" (Matthew 14:35-36).

It is His will to heal all. Everyone who touches Him is made perfectly whole.

"And he came down with them, and stood in the plain, and the company of his disciples, and a great multitude of people, out of all Judea and Jerusalem, and from the seacoast of Tyre and Sidon, who came to hear him and to be healed of their diseases, And they that were vexed with unclean spirits; and they were healed. And the whole multitude sought to touch him; for there went virtue out of him, and HE HEALED THEM ALL" (Luke 6:17-19).

Virtue means "miracle working power." The same word is used when you are filled with the Holy Spirit. You are filled with power. Did you know that you are filled with miracle working power? That's why He said to lay hands on people—so that the miracle working power could come out of you. It wasn't given just to be in you. It is to flow through you. *"And he healed them all."* In His home town He didn't heal many people, but that was because of their unbelief (Mark 6:6).

God's benefit package includes healing for

your physical body. Will you believe it and receive it? *"Who hath believed our report?" (Isaiah 53:1).* Will you say, "I do!"? If you'll believe, the arm of the Lord shall be revealed to you!

For information regarding Marilyn Hickey's monthly Bible reading program, you may write:

OUTPOURING
P.O. Box 17340
Denver, CO 80217

For Prayer, call
888-637-4545

or join us on the worldwide web at:
www.mhmin.org

Books by Marilyn Hickey

Winning Over Weight

Women of the Word

God's Benefit: Healing

Available at your local bookstore.

Harrison House
P. O. Box 35035 • Tulsa, OK 74153